My Prayer for You

Pat Robertson

My Prayer for You

Fleming H. Revell Company
Old Tappan, New Jersey

Library of Congress Cataloging in Publication Data

Robertson, Pat.
   My prayer for you.

   1. Christian life.   I. Title.
BV4501.2.R6155   248′.48′61   77-8607
ISBN 0-8007-0869-5

Contents

Foreword

"Salvation is a gift received in a moment, but we spend all our lives and all eternity unwrapping it." This statement is as true today as it was in the twelfth century when Saint Bernard made it.

In one chapter of *My Prayer for You* Pat Robertson tells us how to receive the gift, and in the rest, how to unwrap the package.

This book is not for everybody. It is not for the spiritual gimmick seeker. Pat will never lead you to believe that overemphasis placed on one truth will bring you to the Promised Land and then leave you stranded.

My Prayer for You unfolds no new revelation. Every truth in it is old, simple, plain, and down to earth. Each is so old it will make you new; so plain it will make you beautiful; so simple it will make you wise; so down to earth it will lift you heavenward.

It *is* for the man who wants to "unwrap" his package and yearns to tap every resource he has in Christ. May the Spirit who anointed Pat to write this, anoint you as you read it. It could make all the difference in your life.

HARALD BREDESEN

My Prayer for You

1
Dominion–
God-Given Authority

Everything was to be under the feet of man, as long as man himself was under the control of God.

What is God's ultimate intention for you? Why did God place you here on earth, and what authority did He give you? To learn God's intention for mankind, we must go back to the Book of Genesis, the book of beginnings.

There we read that God made, as the pinnacle of His creation, a creature formed in His own image—one that was called man. He took some dust from the ground; He breathed life into it, and that creature became a living soul.

What did God intend for that creature He had made in His own image? I believe that He intended man to dwell continuously in His presence. God intended man to hear His voice, to obey His commands, to love Him, to worship Him, to enjoy Him, to walk in fellowship with Him.

We find a description of the Lord walking in the Garden looking for man, desiring to have fellowship with him, to talk to him, to love him.

> And they heard the voice of the Lord God **walk-ing** in the garden in the cool of the day . . . . And the Lord God called unto Adam, and said unto him, Where art thou?
>
> Genesis 3:8, 9

Isn't this really what Jesus Christ is saying in the Book of Revelation with these words:

> Behold, I stand at the door, and knock: if any man hear my voice, and open the door, I will come in to him, and will sup with him, and he with me.
>
> Revelation 3:20

Doesn't this imply fellowship with God? Along with that fellowship comes a family relationship. We are not only made in the image of the Creator, but we are brothers of the Son of God, who is the firstborn of the Father.

If we are brothers of Jesus, we are heirs of God— joint heirs with Christ. As heirs, all things are ours. What used to be, what is going to be, whatever there is, in heaven or in earth, is for us in union with Jesus Christ.

What calling could be higher?

> What is man, that thou art mindful of him? and the son of man, that thou visitest him? For thou

hast made him a little lower than the angels . . .
and madest him to have dominion over all the
works of thy hands . . . .

Psalms 8:4–6

God Almighty has placed us on earth to have dominion over the works of His hands. We were initially to
be a little lower than angels, but through Jesus Christ,
we are above the angels, since we are seated in
heavenly places in Christ Jesus.

So, if you are indeed a born-again Christian, you are
a child of God, a joint heir with Jesus Christ. You are
above all the angels; you are above all created beings;
you are above everything in all of the universe, save
God Himself. You are in union with Christ Jesus and
are part of His body. He is part of you. His Spirit
dwells within you, and you dwell in Him.

And God said, Let us make man in our image,
after our likeness: and let them have dominion
[*dominion* means "lordship"] over the fish of
the sea, and over the fowl of the air, and over
the cattle, and over all the earth, and over every
creeping thing that creepeth upon the earth. So
God created man in his own image, in the image
of God created he him; male and female created
he them. And God blessed them, and God said
unto them, Be fruitful, and multiply, and re-
plenish the earth, and subdue it: and have

dominion over the fish of the sea, and over the
fowl of the air, and over every living thing that
moveth upon the earth. And God said, Behold, I
have given you every herb bearing seed, which
is upon the face of all the earth, and every tree,
in the which is the fruit of a tree yielding seed;
to you it shall be for meat . . . . And God saw
every thing that he had made, and, behold, it
was very good . . . .

Genesis 1:26–29, 31

God's intention is very clearly stated. God placed
mankind on earth to have dominion, and every other
being on earth was to be subject to man, as long as
man himself was under the control of God. But in
order to have fellowship with the Creator, it is necessary to be yielded to the Creator. When man began to
rebel against the wishes of his Creator, then he no
longer had authority and dominion.

An alien power, whom we call Lucifer, the light
one; Satan, the adversary; Apollyon, the devil (he has
many names) invaded this planet. In order for him to
have any effectiveness, he had to work through one of
the creatures that God placed here. He chose to work
through the serpent, the snake. The serpent was the
most subtle of all creatures, but man had dominion
over the serpent. All man had to say was, "Snake, be
quiet. Leave me alone," and the snake would have to
obey him.

Instead of rebuking this creature and sending it away, the woman began to talk with it. The first words that the snake uttered cast doubt on the truthfulness and goodness of God: ". . . Yea, hath God said . . . ?" (Genesis 3:1).

You may say, "Well, what's so wrong with that?" If I came to you and asked, "Is your husband really faithful?" what does that do? Anything that casts doubt on the goodness of another person is devastating.

Instead of rebuking the serpent and stopping it the first minute, the woman began to talk back to it:

And the woman said unto the serpent, We may eat of the fruit of the trees of the garden: But of the fruit of the tree which is in the midst of the garden, God hath said, Ye shall not eat of it, neither shall ye touch it, lest ye die.

Genesis 3:2, 3

At that point, it seemed to Eve as if the gracious Word of God were somehow arbitrary, somehow selfish. And the serpent came back to her immediately, saying:

. . . Ye shall not surely die: For God doth know that in the day ye eat thereof, then your eyes shall be opened, and ye shall be as gods . . . .

Genesis 3:4, 5

The woman then looked at that fruit and saw that it was something desirable, which would make people wise, and so she ate it. Later she gave some to her husband. In eating the forbidden fruit, man sinned, man fell, man no longer was in fellowship with God. Man lost the dominion which God had given him over this earth.

The serpent has not changed his techniques over the years. His solicitation, time and time again, is that there is something desirable which God wants to hold back from man. He says certain drugs are useful in giving a person an understanding of the spiritual life. He says that alcohol is good in making man joyful. He tells man that forbidden sex is pleasant and that God is merely trying to repress man.

The lies continue, but they are always the same pattern: God desires to keep something from you. As long as man will continue to believe the lie of the serpent, man will continue to be in bondage to a creature that God has placed in man's power. You and I were intended to have dominion. You and I were intended to be free. God does not wish any of His people to be in bondage to anything.

When you trace back through history, you will find that satanic activity centers on bringing men and women into bondage. Recall the demon-possessed men of the past—Adolf Hitler, Joseph Stalin, Karl Marx—leaders who have subjugated millions of people in the name of a political system.

Where satanic activity is at work, there will be bondage. There will be fear. There will be rules and regulations, strict discipline, and an attempt to take away the joy and freedom of the individual. The various types of lusts that plague mankind are all an attempt by the enemy to take authority over us, even though he knows that we, as children of God, have a mandate from God to take dominion over *him*.

When Jesus came to earth, He reestablished the authority that was lost by Adam and Eve. He once again gave to His people power over all nature, all disease, and over all the works of the enemy.

Jesus once sent out a certain few of His disciples on a ministry of preaching.

And the seventy returned again with joy, saying, Lord, even the devils are subject unto us through thy name. And he said unto them, I beheld Satan as lightning fall from heaven. Behold, I give unto you power to tread on serpents and scorpions, and over all the power of the enemy . . . .

Luke 10:17–19

This is restoration of the Christian's mandate. No Christian should ever fear Satan. No Christian should be in bondage to anything, especially to Satan. There should be no bondage to the occult: to horoscopes, Ouija boards, or witchcraft. There should be no fear of

magic amulets, black cats, curses, witches, and the
other trappings of the occult. We should never fear the
enemy, or even discuss him. We have victory over
him.

Jesus has said: "I have restored the power and the
dominion which man lost" (see Matthew 18:11). If you
belong to God, then as His child, you have authority
over all the power of the enemy. Just before Jesus
Christ ascended into heaven, He gave a commission
to His people:

> And Jesus came and spake unto them, saying,
> All power is given unto me in heaven and in
> earth. Go ye therefore, and teach all nations,
> baptizing them in the name of the Father, and of
> the Son, and of the Holy Ghost: Teaching them
> to observe all things whatsoever I have com-
> manded you: and, lo, I am with you alway, even
> unto the end of the world. Amen.
>
>   Matthew 28:18–20

My Lord, You have given Your people authority over all
the power of the enemy. For You said, Lord Jesus, that all
authority, all power in heaven and earth, is given to You.
Even as we are to go forth in Your name to take the Gospel
throughout this world, You in turn are giving us the authority and power that we need.

We pray for those who love You, asking You to give to
them power and authority over all the work of the enemy.

We pray that You will break the shackles of any satanic power that binds them. We pray that the glory of God and the praise of God will be upon them, and will fill their lips as they worship You and have fellowship with You in freedom from all bondage.

Thank You, Father, for hearing. Thank You for answering this prayer. In the name of Jesus.

This is my prayer for you.

2

Commanded to Be Filled With the Spirit

All that is necessary is that we surrender ourselves in faith to Jesus Christ and ask Him as Baptizer to baptize us in the Holy Spirit.

Have you ever wanted power in your life? Have you wanted to be effective as a witness for Jesus Christ? Have you desired the ability to move people closer to your Saviour?

Most Christians have wanted these things. Many of you have heard about Baptism of the Holy Spirit, or the Fullness of the Spirit, and you have wanted that experience.

I know some of you are frightened by the idea. After all, anything dealing with the supernatural can be a little frightening. Unfortunately, in the King James Bible, the word *spirit* has been translated "ghost." We think of supernatural spirits, and we're frightened by them.

We need not be frightened. The Spirit of God is a Spirit of love, of warmth, of joy. He is a Spirit of praise, a Spirit who brings us into the knowledge and the presence of Jesus. The Spirit of God brings about love, long-suffering, patience, gentleness, and goodness. There's nothing frightening about those things, is there? This isn't some ghost who runs around in an old sheet—this is the Spirit of God Himself!

Jesus Christ knew that His disciples were power-less. Some of them were cowardly. Some were doubt-ing. Others were vying for power and prestige, while a few others seemed to have complete spiritual dead-ness and a lack of perception. Jesus had quite a few problems with His disciples.

He knew that if He sent this group of men out into the Roman world, they were doomed to fail. He didn't dare send them forth in their condition, because they were weak and sinful. So, as He departed from them, He gave them strict instructions to remain in Jerusalem until they were endued with power from on high.

> For John truly baptized with water; but ye shall be baptized with the Holy Ghost not many days hence.
>
> Acts 1:5

After their baptism, He assured them, they would be capable:

> But ye shall receive power, after that the Holy Ghost is come upon you: and ye shall be wit-nesses unto me both in Jerusalem, and in all of Judea, and in Samaria, and unto the uttermost part of the earth.
>
> Acts 1:8

This is exactly what those disciples needed to hear. They were a group of frightened, confused, uneducated men with no wealth, no prestige, no big churches, no organizational structure—none of the things people consider essential to carry out a mission.

Yet, Jesus told them to go into all the world and preach the Gospel. They were faced with an alien and hostile environment, and yet they knew that their mission would succeed. Jesus also knew it would succeed, because He was going to the Father and was going to send down the blessed Holy Spirit. The Spirit would be a Comforter to the disciples—He would come with strength. He would be beside them as an Advocate, as a friend, and as One who would endue them with all the power they would need.

And when the day of Pentecost was fully come, they were all with one accord in one place. And suddenly there came a sound from heaven as of a rushing mighty wind, and it filled all the house where they were sitting. And there appeared unto them cloven tongues like as of fire, and it sat upon each of them. And they were all filled with the Holy Ghost, and began to speak with other tongues, as the Spirit gave them utterance.

Acts 2:1–4

What a fabulous revelation from God! Suddenly simple fishermen, a tax collector, and others who had joined themselves to Jesus were empowered from on high.

And they began to do something that natural people cannot do. They began to speak clearly in other languages, so that Persians, Mesopotamians, Elamites, Parthians, and people from all over the Roman Empire were able to understand clearly, in their own language, the mighty acts of God.

These disciples were not preaching the Gospel in tongues, but they were magnifying and extolling God. Of course, people said, "They're drunk." But Peter replied:

> For these are not drunken, as ye suppose, seeing it is but the third hour of the day. But this is that which was spoken by the prophet Joel; And it shall come to pass in the last days, saith God, I will pour out of my Spirit upon all flesh: and your sons and your daughters shall prophesy, and your young men shall see visions, and your old men shall dream dreams.
>
> Acts 2:15–17

This was the promise of the Father that Jesus said He would send to His disciples. This group of men was suddenly transformed into men who walked like supermen on the face of the earth. They were so changed that in some cities, men trembled when they came to them and said they were men who turned the world upside down (*see* Acts 17:6).

It's small wonder that they conquered the Roman Empire. A task that seemed absolutely certain to fail suddenly looked like it was absolutely certain to succeed, because the disciples had become endued with power from on high.

Some of you may say, "Yes, but is this for me? Perhaps it was for the early disciples only. What about right now?"

Well, what about right now? Peter said:

> For the promise is unto you, and to your children, and to all that are afar off, even as many as the Lord our God shall call.
>
> Acts 2:39

This experience is not optional—it is absolutely crucial in the life of every Christian. As a matter of fact, Paul commanded:

> And be not drunk with wine, wherein is excess; but be filled with the Spirit.
>
> Ephesians 5:18

Christians are *commanded* to be filled with the Spirit. God will not command something that He Himself will not perform. He does not direct us to seek a level of spiritual life which He will deny to us. God does not act capriciously with His children. If He directs us to be filled with the Holy Spirit, then we *shall* be filled with the Holy Spirit!

If you have desired more of God, if you have wanted more of His power, this in itself is a promise of its own fulfillment. Of course, the average human being does not really want God; he wants more of self, not more of God. But if you begin to hunger and thirst after righteousness, Jesus Christ has said, "You will be fulfilled. You will be filled to overflowing with righteousness" (*see* Matthew 5:6). If you desire this blessing, know for sure that the desire has come from God. It has not come from you, because God Almighty placed it in your heart. That desire is a promise of its own fulfillment.

You may ask, "How do I receive this blessing? What must I do?"

An analogy can be made with baptism. John said that he baptized with water, but One was coming after him who would baptize with the Holy Spirit and fire.

In Christian baptism, there is a baptizer—normally a clergyman—who will perform the rite. There is the element of baptism, which is water, and there is a candidate for baptism.

In certain fellowships, the candidate walks down into the water, which is the element, then the baptizer places that person into the water, or submerges him, and brings him up again. While doing this, he says a

prayer, reads a Scripture, or brings some type of blessing and benediction. This is considered a valid baptism.

When we move from physical baptism to spiritual
baptism, we find that Jesus Christ is the Baptizer.
Jesus takes the candidate and places him in the element.

When we have received Jesus Christ as our Saviour
and have been washed by Him and have asked Him to
come and live as our Lord, at that moment, the Holy
Spirit comes and lives within us.

We use the term *Christ is in my heart,* but what we
are actually describing is the process where the Spirit
of Christ, the Holy Spirit, has come to live in our
hearts. There He reproduces in us the life of Jesus:
love, joy, peace, long-suffering, patience, goodness,
gentleness—what we call the fruits of the Holy Spirit.
In the Baptism of the Holy Spirit, Jesus Christ as Baptizer takes us as the candidates and places us into the
glorious waters of the Holy Spirit and fire.

As a minister, I have baptized a number of people. I
can assure you that it helps me not one bit if the individual displays physical manifestations. The only
thing they have to do is stand quietly in the water, and
I will perform the baptism.

So it is in the Baptism of the Holy Spirit. All that is
necessary is that we surrender ourselves in faith to
Jesus Christ and ask Him as Baptizer to baptize us in
the Holy Spirit. We surrender ourselves to Him; we

ask Him; we believe in Him; then we take the Holy
Spirit by faith as our possession, and He does the
rest.

As we look at the Bible, especially the Book of Acts,
we notice that in each recorded incident of a Baptism
of the Holy Spirit, there was an accompanying physical manifestation—speaking in a heavenly or an un-
known language.

I believe, although there is no specific teaching on
this, that it would be considered the norm in the New
Testament experience for the candidate for Baptism of
the Holy Spirit to speak in another language when this
blessing came upon him.

> . . . and began to speak with other tongues, as
> the Spirit gave them utterance.
>
> Acts 2:4

I would like to pray for you to be filled with the
Holy Spirit. As I pray for you, I want you to look to
Jesus and surrender yourself completely to Him as
your Baptizer. I want you to expect to receive this
blessing. And I wish, if you would, that you would
begin to worship Him and to tell Him you love Him.
Don't ask more than once. Then I want you to receive
and begin to worship Him. As there comes forth a
beautiful, heavenly language, speak it forth in love,
even as in the Book of Acts, unto the Lord.

Heavenly Father, at this moment we come to You. We pray that the Holy Spirit might come upon these praying. Lord Jesus, baptize those who are praying now in the Holy Spirit, with Your power and Your love.

My brother, my sister, in Jesus' name be filled with His power. Receive the Baptism of His Spirit at this very moment. May the anointing, may the glory, may the power of God come into your life.

Thank You, Father, that You have heard our prayer. Thank You for granting this blessing. Thank You for what You have done in this life.

This, my friend, is my prayer for you.

Reaching millions daily through 700 Club TV and radio broadcasts, host Pat Robertson discusses personal commitments to Christ with entertainers, authors, politicians, and business persons. This interview with President Jimmy Carter was broadcast over more than 150 TV and radio stations nationwide. *Left:* Never one to sit back, Pat pitches in at the 700 Club Counseling Center, where volunteers lend help and support to problem-burdened viewers who call in. The response has been so great that each major city where the show is aired has its own counseling center.

The late Kathryn Kuhlman, the Spirit-filled healer, assisted during one of the 700 Club telethons.

Charles Colson (center left) and Eldridge Cleaver (center right), once inimically opposed in their political beliefs, now as forcefully joined in their commitment to Christ, gave Pat and cohost Ben Kinchlow one of the most powerful interviews in 700 Club history. *Below:* As proof of answered prayer, Christian Broadcasting Network radio has come a long way from this Chesapeake, Virginia, garage in 1962.

Pat shows off plans for CBN's International Communications Center. The center will include two 10,000-square-foot TV broadcasting studios, a communications college which will eventually train about 2,000 American and international students a year, a satellite earth station, an international language translation facility, an international counseling center, a theological college, a twenty-four-hour prayer center, a library, a motel, three dormitories, a 2,400-seat convention hall, and a nondenominational school of theology.

Just as the journey of a thousand miles begins with one step, Dede Robertson, Pat's wife, takes the first shovelful of earth, signaling the start of construction on the extensive center. From left to right are CBN board members Pat, Dede, the Reverend Harald Bredesen, Bob G. Slosser, and S. Tucker Yates.

Going beyond the typical groundbreaking ceremonies, Pat puts in gear CBN's far-reaching program to evangelize the world as he starts a pile driver at the construction site. With him are (left to right) M. R. Welch, foundation contractor, Dede Robertson, and the Reverend Harald Bredesen.

Representatives of the five continents, symbolizing CBN's planned worldwide evangelism outreach from Virginia Beach, erect a cross during groundbreaking ceremonies for the center.

Becoming the first Christian ministry to build and operate its own satellite earth station, CBN jumped ahead in the communications field, as one step of the new center was completed.

Chinese evangelist Nora Lam urges viewers to freely give as they have freely received during a 700 Club Telethon. CBN missionary funds have been used to reach the entire nation of Taiwan through Nora Lam's evangelistic crusades in Taipei.

This recent West Coast Telethon "sealed CBN as a nationwide voice," according to Pat.

3
There Is Only One Answer

What reason can you give Me to come spend eternity with Me in what is called heaven?

I am going to tell you the greatest secret of all the universe. It's a secret that Jesus Christ told to a ruler of the Jews whose name was Nicodemus. Nicodemus, an elder in Israel, came to Jesus by night to ask Him for secrets. He said to Jesus, ". . . Rabbi, we know that thou art a teacher come from God . . ." (John 3:2).

Nicodemus, who had achieved eminence among his people, wanted to know something more about God. He wanted to know how he could touch heaven. He wanted to know how he could see God.

Nicodemus assumed that the way to get that revelation was to be taught about it. He thought if he could have more instruction, he would be ushered into the presence of God, and he would know more about God.

In Hebrew thought, knowledge was not something you learned only from a book. Knowledge was also gained when you lived intimately with someone for many years. This is the kind of knowledge that Nicodemus wanted. He wanted the knowledge of an intimate relationship with his Creator.

You can imagine his shock when Jesus said, ". . . Except a man be born again, he cannot see the kingdom of God" (John 3:3).

"What do you mean, *born again?*" Nicodemus replied. "Do you mean to tell me that a man of my age would have to enter back into his mother's womb as an embryo and be born all over again?" (*See* John 3:4.)

Jesus answered, "That's right. You must be born again. But I'm not talking about the kind of birth that you had as a physical being. I'm talking about something else" (*see* John 3:5). He continued: ". . . Except a man be born of water and of the Spirit, he cannot enter into the kingdom of God" (John 3:5).

You can imagine the incredulous look on the face of Nicodemus. He couldn't believe such a thing. All his life, he'd been taught that good works were the key to heaven—that if you observed all of the laws and requirements of God, you would have entrance into heaven.

Then came this unusual teacher, who was clearly a man of God, who clearly knew God in the most intimate way, and He told Nicodemus he must be born again. He couldn't understand.

Jesus could see the look on his face, and He said, "Nicodemus, you're a ruler of your people; you're a teacher. Don't you understand? If you can't understand earthly things, how then can I teach you about heavenly things, which is what you really want to know? Look around you, and you will see what I mean. Do you see the wind?" (*See* John 3:10–12.)

Jesus continued: "Do you know the wind? You don't know where it's coming from; you don't know where it's going; but you can see its effects. You can see what it does to the trees. You can see the leaves that are caught up in the wind. You can see the little swirls of dust. You can feel the wind on your face. It's like that with those who are born of the Spirit" (*see* John 3:8).

No, you can't see how it happens. You can't see the process that is going on inside those people, but you can know that something has happened. You can see their acts, hear their speech, and feel the love and compassion that flows forth from those who have been born of the Spirit.

The problem was, Nicodemus was of the flesh. He was from the earth, and that's earthy. Flesh is mortal. It is subject to death, decay, and corruption. It is filled with self-pity, self-pride, self-love. Flesh is consumed, in its basic being, with evil.

As David said: ". . . I was shapen in iniquity . . ." (Psalms 51:5). Sin is implicit in every one of us. There is sin in the depths of our being. Sin is intertwined with the very best of us. We call it original sin; the nature of Adam. It describes you; it describes me; it describes all men.

> For all have sinned, and come short of the glory of God.
>
> Romans 3:23

None of us wants to think that we are in the crowd.
We prefer to think that we are special. But the popes,
the bishops, the evangelists—all these have been
sinners—along with us.

There has been but one good man in all the world,
and that was Jesus Christ. He was the only One who
did not need to be born again.

We were made from the base elements—iron, cop-
per, cobalt, calcium—worth very little in themselves.
That which partakes of the dust of the ground is not
very valuable.

In addition, in you and me is a desire to fulfill our
own end. We desire to fulfill *our* lives, *our* dreams,
our successes—sometimes on our own, but always at
the expense of our relationship with God.

> The wicked . . . go astray as soon as they be
> born, speaking lies.
>
> Psalms 58:3

We can cover our nature with a veneer of righteousness. We can go to church, month after month, and
listen to sermons. We can belong to Sunday-school
classes or teach. We can give to various religious
causes. There are many things we can do that seem
righteous, but there is no way that we can eradicate
our inner natures.

There is no way, in our own works and our own
strength, that we can eliminate the substance that we

received at birth. Nicodemus couldn't do it. None of us can.

Except a man be born again, he cannot see the kingdom of heaven. God's ways are not our ways. His thoughts are not our thoughts. There is only one way we can look into that heavenly vision, and that is to be born again.

Assume for a moment that you died, and your spirit, which is immortal, is carried into the presence of your Creator. There you stand, stripped of all your possessions, all your friends, and all your accomplishments.

He looks at you with love, with compassion, and yet with a sense of total, holy, righteous judgment, and He says to you in that awesome moment: "What reason can you give Me to come and spend eternity with Me, in what is called heaven?"

Some of you would say, "Why, I've been a member of the church for thirty years." Others would say, "I have been good. I have fostered public activities. I have given to the church. I have loved my fellow-man."

You could go on and on, and in each instance, God would shake His head and say, "I'm sorry. I love you, but I cannot have you in heaven with Me. You are relying on your good works, and by the works of the flesh shall no man be justified."

There's only one answer to God's question: "I have been born again of the Spirit of God."

You ask, "Well, what do I do to be born again? Is it some magical process?"

No—it's so simple, a little child can do it. Yet, it's so complex that the greatest scholars couldn't figure all of the love that God has put into making this plan available.

In order to be born again, you must recognize that you are a sinner, that you need to be born again, and cannot make it on your own. You must turn from pride, which says, "I am sufficient in myself."

You must turn to the One who is talking to Nicodemus—Jesus of Nazareth, the Son of God. You must recognize that He died to pay the price for your sins. He died on a cruel cross, having been beaten, having been spat upon, having a crown of thorns pressed into His brow, having rough nails driven into His hands and feet. You must recognize this One was the Son of God. He died to pay the price for you. God made Him to be sin, who knew no sin, so that you might become the righteousness of God in Him.

You must believe that He rose again from the grave. He ascended into heaven, free from sin, having left behind the burden He'd taken from all of us. You must believe that He lives now, to be your Lord and Saviour.

Then, if you will turn from your old way, from the pride and self-seeking that is part of you and me, turn to Him and say: "Jesus, I take You as my Saviour and my Lord. Come now and take charge of my life. Send

Your Holy Spirit to live within me, that I might be born of the Spirit of God."

At that moment, dear friend, if you truly receive and believe, Jesus will enter in. He will give you a brand-new life. He will give you new joy, new hope, and everlasting life.

Would you like to do that right now? I know you would. I don't believe you would say no to Jesus if you would think of what He has done for you.

I am going to pray a prayer with you. If you pray from the depths of your heart, and mean it sincerely, Jesus Christ will come into your life, and you will be born again. Say these words from your heart:

> Lord Jesus, I am a sinner. Lord, I have not lived for You, but for myself. I turn away now from the sin of my life and my own selfishness, and I turn to You. I believe that You died for my sins, that You rose again that I might live with You forever. Lord Jesus, I receive You as my Saviour and my Lord. Take my life, Jesus, and make it Your own. Thank You, Lord, for hearing my prayer.

Father, for those who have prayed that prayer with me, may the power of the Holy Spirit of God come into their lives. Fill them, Lord, with Your power, in Jesus' name. *Amen* and *Amen.*

God bless you.

4

By Your Stripes
We Are Healed

**Christ did not die just to save your soul
from sin. He also died that He might bring
healing to your body.**

Do you suppose God wants to heal cancer, heart trouble, strokes, diabetes, arthritis? Is it God's will to heal the physical body, or is this something that passed away with the early church?

I feel that the Bible teaches it is God's perfect will to heal the spirit, soul, and the body. I'm going to talk to you about how you can be healed according to the will of God. I'm going to pray with you, that God Almighty will reach out and bring healing to you or your loved one.

Let's begin with the question that most people ask: "Is it truly God's will to heal?" I've been to many meetings where people prayed, "O God, please heal my friend who is suffering from cancer, if it be Thy will." Then another time they pray: "O God, my friend is lying in the hospital, suffering from a heart attack. Heal him, if it be Thy will."

I feel that this type of prayer doesn't accomplish anything, because it is totally lacking in faith, and God desires a prayer of faith.

But you ask, "Isn't that the way we're supposed to pray—'. . . if it be Thy will'?" If we don't know what God's will is, then yes, we should pray that. None of us should demand things from God. None of us should come before God Almighty and insist that He do something, unless we *know* that the thing we request is indeed His will.

What is the will of God concerning physical healing? The Lord Jesus Christ gave us a model prayer—the Lord's Prayer. In it, we are told to pray: "Our Father, who art in heaven, Hallowed be thy name. Thy kingdom come. Thy will be done on earth, as it is in heaven."

Let's contemplate heaven for a moment. From what we learn in the Bible, heaven is a place of eternal joy, of eternal bliss; a place where there is no sorrow, death, tears, or sickness. It is a place where the spirits of the redeemed, filled with joy and praise, live in the presence of the holy God.

There is such prosperity in heaven that they use the precious metals of earth for paving stones. Heaven exceeds the wildest imaginations of any of us.

. . . Eye hath not seen, nor ear heard, neither have entered into the heart of man, the things which God hath prepared for them that love him.

1 Corinthians 2:9

Could you picture a heaven filled with crutches, wheelchairs, the blind, and the lame? Could you conceive of men and women with their hands twisted from the ravages of arthritis, or their bodies eaten with wasting cancer? Could you conceive of heaven that way? Of course not!

Why do you think it's God's will for earth to be that way? I believe it is the perfect will of our Father in heaven that we who are His children should prosper and be in health, even as our souls prosper. God takes delight in the prosperity of His servants.

If God is a merciful heavenly Father, I must of necessity believe that He is more merciful than any human father. I find it hard to believe that a human father would take pleasure in seeing his child crippled, maimed, halt, or diseased. And I cannot conceive that it would ever be the will of God that human beings should be sick and diseased.

The Bible says that Jesus went about healing all who were oppressed of the devil. As a matter of fact, if you look carefully into the life of Jesus Christ, who was the perfect representation of God on earth, you will find not one single instance when He turned down someone who came to Him for physical healing.

I cannot recall even one prayer in which Jesus turned to the Father and said, "Father, heal this one, *if it be Thy will.*"

Once a leper came to Him and said, "Lord, if You will, You can make me clean." Jesus reached forth a hand of compassion, touched him, and said, ". . . I will; be thou clean . . ." (Matthew 8:3).

We read in Mark's Gospel: ". . . they brought unto him all that were diseased, and them that were possessed with devils . . . . And he healed many that were sick . . . and cast out many devils . . ." (Mark 1:32, 34).

I know of no instance when Jesus Christ failed to heal a sick person. Was He not the perfect will of God? Of course He was. Did He ever sin? No, He didn't. Didn't He always hear the voice of the Father? Of course He did. Did He walk in the will of God? Certainly He did. Is it the will of God to heal you right now? Yes, it is.

What is the basis of our healing? How can someone be bold enough to say that God desires to heal you of a physical condition? Perhaps the doctors have said the condition cannot be healed.

I have run into quite a few cases like that, in which medical science has done all that is possible. I appreciate medical science. I believe that doctors and modern medicine are a gift of God to mankind. I hope that God will give us cures for some of the terrible wasting diseases that afflict mankind. Every breakthrough in medical science is a blessing for all of mankind.

Yet, there are times when doctors have done all they can do and must say, "The condition is hopeless. This condition will get worse, and the patient will die."

Does that mean that death must invariably come?

Of course it doesn't; because there is a Great Physician, One greater than medical science. There is a power greater than all of man's science and technology. No doctor has ever healed anybody. The doctor can bind the wound, sew the cut, pour in the antibiotic, or give the injection; but only God Almighty can heal.

If He decides to heal, then it will be done. But, how? Why? What is the righteous basis on which God heals? I would like to cite several verses from the Book of the Prophet Isaiah, which will give you an understanding of the ground on which we base a prayer for your healing.

> All we like sheep have gone astray; we have turned every one to his own way; and the Lord hath laid on him the iniquity of us all. He was oppressed, and he was afflicted, yet he opened not his mouth: he is brought as a lamb to the slaughter, and as a sheep before her shearers is dumb, so he openeth not his mouth. He was taken from prison and from judgment: and who shall declare his generation? for he was cut off out of the land of the living: for the transgression of my people was he stricken.
>
> Isaiah 53:6–8

The prophet was referring to the death of Jesus Christ for our sins. The iniquities and the transgres-

sions that every one of us has committed were all
taken away by the death of Jesus Christ. He was the
righteous sacrifice for every one of us. So, if you know
Jesus, if you have truly been born again, if you are a
child of God, you can base your hope of forgiveness
and salvation on a finished work that was done by
Jesus Christ on the cross.

The prophet also wrote:

> Surely he hath borne our griefs, and carried our
> sorrows: yet we did esteem him stricken, smit-
> ten of God, and afflicted. But he was wounded
> for our transgressions, he was bruised for our
> iniquities: the chastisement of our peace was
> upon him; and with his stripes we are healed.
>
> Isaiah 53:4, 5

The two words, *griefs* and *sorrows*, literally mean
"sickness" and "pains." Jesus did not die just to save
your soul from sin. He also died that He might bring
healing to your body.

If you review in your mind events of that awful day
we call Good Friday, you remember that Jesus Christ
was tried before Pontius Pilate, then surrendered to
the Roman soldiers to be scourged. You read the word
scourged, and it doesn't have much impact on you,
until you realize that they took Jesus Christ, the Son of
God, and tied Him to a concrete pillar. They stripped
the clothes from His back. Then He was handed over
to a Roman legionnaire, a man with little or no moral

convictions, a man used to brutality and violence, a man of coarseness and brute strength. They gave this man a cat-o'-nine-tails—a whip that had nine thongs with a little metal pellet at the end of each of the thongs.

The scourging was what the Jews called *the near death;* forty lashes less one; thirty-nine stripes. As the Son of God, who was already weakened from fasting and interrogation, was held to that concrete column, the muscular arm of the legionnaire rose and fell, and those stripes came across the back of Jesus Christ.

Once again, the arm was raised, the soldier gritted his teeth, and again, the lash whistled through the air. *Smack!* Into the back of Jesus Christ! Again and again the cruel arm was raised and brought down, with all of its force, upon the back of a suffering Saviour.

Little bits of flesh tore loose, and red welts developed. The lash came down again and again. The skin was torn off, and then the flesh was opened up, perhaps all the way to the bone. The white of the bones began to show, but the red blood was now pouring out of those cuts on the back of our Saviour. They called them stripes, for they looked as if somebody had painted them on His back. But it wasn't paint—it was the blood of our Saviour.

The Bible says: "By those stripes you are healed." I am healed. We *are* healed—not *will be* healed, not *may be* healed—we *are* healed.

This is one of the great affirmations of the Scripture,

repeated also by the apostle Peter in the New Testament. "That by the stripes of Jesus Christ we have been made whole" (*see* 1 Peter 2:24).

What was the whipping for? What part did it play? Was this some idle amusement that the heavenly Father permitted His Son to endure? Did He take fiendish pleasure in prolonging the agony of Jesus? He would have died just as surely on the cross without the stripes. The nails and the crucifixion were enough to bring about death, and by His death we are saved. By His death our iniquity has been pardoned, our transgressions forgiven. Why, then, the stripes?

I submit to you that the reason for that terrible torture of our Saviour was to bring about physical healing in your life—now—today. Is it the will of God to heal? If it wasn't the will of God, why did Jesus Christ suffer for our healing? Why has the price been paid?

Wholeness came as part of His atoning sacrifice. There would be no sickness without sin; no death without sin and sickness. They all fall together, don't they? Sin, sickness, death—they all are together. Not that any specific sin brings about a specific sickness, but because there is sin and transgression in the human race, there is also sickness, and there is death.

If Jesus Christ came to take away sin and the consequence of sin, which is death, He also came to take away sickness. If a man can stand totally in the presence of Almighty God, he will not be sick. He will not

have illness in his life, nor can he have death, because
he is totally in God's presence.

Because of what Scripture says, I feel confident that
I can pray for you, and as we join together in prayer,
God will reach out His hand and bring healing to you,
if you will trust Him.

> . . . That if two of you shall agree on earth as
> touching any thing that they shall ask, it shall be
> done for them of my Father which is in heaven.
>
> Matthew 18:19

I believe at this moment, you and I can agree together on earth. Though distance separates us, there is
no separation of the love of God and His Spirit. I believe if you kneel at this moment, and ask God to bring
healing to your body, you will find that by the stripes
of Jesus, you have already been healed.

As you are kneeling and expecting the answer on
the basis of the Word of God, on His clear promises,
and even clearer work on the cross for you, I am going
to pray. If you will pray with me and receive from
Him, I believe that at this moment you will receive
healing in your body.

My heavenly Father, I pray for this dear one who at this
very moment is praying with me. I believe, God, that on the
stripes of Jesus were placed the physical maladies that have

plagued the human race for so long. I believe by Your atoning sacrifice, Father, You took these things upon Yourself;
that by Your stripes we are healed.

So at this moment, I speak the word of faith that would
bring healing in the name of Jesus. I agree with my dear
friend, now praying with me, and together we claim Your
promises and speak the word of faith.

My dear friend, in the name of Jesus, be made whole.
May His healing grace come into your life at this moment.
Be whole in the name of Jesus. Father, we thank You, and
we give You the glory, in Jesus' name. *Amen.*

This, my dear friend, is my prayer for you.

5
Great Is Your Faith

It isn't an increase of your faith that you need; it's an exercise of the true faith that comes from God Almighty.

One day the disciples of Jesus came to Him and made this request: ". . . Lord, Increase our faith" (Luke 17:5). Why did they ask this of Jesus?

They asked because they had seen all manner of wonderful things done by their Lord during His ministry. They had personally seen Jesus Christ raise the dead. They had watched Him still storms. The disciples realized that Jesus Christ had faith, and that His faith was the key to His miracles.

The faith that Jesus Christ exercised opened a whole new realm of experience for the disciples. They entered into a world understood by few people—a world of supernatural reality, where miracles occurred in a commonplace fashion.

The Lord they served had supreme faith, and their faith seemed so small by comparison that they came to Him and asked Him for more faith.

Jesus' answer to that request surprised the disciples:

   . . . If ye had faith as a grain of mustard seed, ye
   might say unto this sycamine tree, Be thou

plucked up by the root, and be thou planted in
the sea; and it should obey you.

Luke 17:6

What was Jesus saying to them? What kind of faith
was He talking about? Jesus was talking about *God's*
faith, not the disciples'.

They had said, "Increase *our* faith," and Jesus answered them, "If you had a mustard seed of true faith,
God's faith, then basically nothing would be impossible for you."

You and I are much like those disciples. We behold
the wonder of Jesus Christ, and see the miraculous
work that He did, then we read, ". . . He that be-
lieveth on me . . . greater works than these shall he
do; because I go unto my Father" (John 14:12).

If we truly love Him and have faith in the Bible,
then we yearn for the opportunity to see such
miraculous things happen in our lives. We find ourselves praying, like the disciples, for more faith.

Yet, every time we ask, we hear Jesus say, "It isn't
an increase of your faith that you need, it's an exercise
of the true faith that comes from God Almighty."

I am amused when I contemplate what the con-
sequences would have been if Jesus had answered
that prayer of the disciples and given them a large
measure of God's faith. They would have had the
power to take the planets out of their orbits! They

would have had so much power that they would have been extremely dangerous. They simply didn't need that much faith. They needed to perceive what was already there and to understand it.

Faith is the only one of the attributes of the Holy Spirit which is listed as both a *fruit* and a *gift* of the Holy Spirit.

Fruit is something that grows. I have a number of apple trees, and in the springtime they have beautiful blossoms. After the blossoms fall, the fruit is formed. A little green bud appears, then grows and grows until it becomes a full-size green apple. As it matures, the apple turns a rosy red or a yellow, golden color, and soon it is ready to eat.

If faith is a *fruit,* then the exercise of that faith will produce a ripe, mature faith. It will grow from a little bud, becoming something large and significant.

On the other hand, faith is also listed as a *gift* of the Holy Spirit. A *gift* is something that comes to you ready-made. People don't give little green apple buds. They wait for the apples to grow in their beauty and succulent taste, and then they pick them and give them. When God makes a gift of faith, this giving becomes a supernatural enablement, full-grown and ready to use.

This means that someone who never walked the way of the Lord, perhaps never served Him and never saw His power—someone who is just starting out as what we call a babe in Christ—can indeed be given a

gift of faith. Through this gift, he could speak a word
and turn back a hurricane. He could summon protect-
ing angels to give physical safety. He could bring
about a change in government merely by prayer. He
could do any of these, if God, at that moment, made a
gift of faith.

You might ask, "What is faith?" I think that is a good
question—what is it? The Bible does a very good job
in defining faith.

> Now faith is the assurance of things hoped for,
> the conviction [or the evidence] of things not
> seen.
>
> Hebrews 11:1 RSV

Faith is the assurance of things that are hoped for.
You are hoping that such and such will happen. You
are hoping for circumstances, for ability, for finances,
for healing. You are hoping for something that is
pragmatic, practical, or visible.

The Greek word for *things* is the same word from
which we get our word *pragmatic*. I want something I
can see and touch, but right now all I have is hope. I'm
hoping for it, but I don't have it before me.

The Bible says that faith is *hupŏstasis*, a Greek
word that means "what stands underneath" (the sub-
stratum, the confidence, the assurance, or, in one instance, the exact nature). Faith is an exact replica of
the thing that you're looking for. It is the underlying

stratum. It is something that goes before it, something that is a mirror image of what you're hoping for.

The Bible tells us that Jesus Christ is the exact replica of God. The Bible uses exactly the same word, *hupŏstasis,* to describe the relationship of Jesus Christ to God the Father. The Word of God, Jesus Christ, is the mirror image of the invisible God.

In the same way, faith is the mirror image of what you're hoping for. If what you hope for becomes concrete in your mind, your spirit, and your heart, it begins to have substance. Then, Jesus Christ says, you will have what you hope for.

Jesus said that if you do not doubt, you can say to the mountain, "Be removed and cast into the sea," and it will obey you.

But why will it obey you? Because hope forms in your spirit; a hope which is clothed with substance; and that substance is faith.

Where does that substance come from? It comes from God. It has to be *God's* faith.

The apostle Paul spoke of living his life by the faith of the Son of God, who loved Paul and gave Himself for him. We are told in the Bible that Jesus is ". . . the author and finisher of our faith . . ." (Hebrews 12:2).

Faith begins in Jesus; it is complete in Jesus. This eliminates the need for you and me to struggle to gain greater faith. Faith is the assurance, the confidence, the superstructure. Faith is the real nature of what it is we're hoping for.

Hebrews 11:1 continues by saying that faith is the evidence, or the conviction, of things not seen. The Greek word used here is the same word that would be used in proving a case in court.

When you try a case, you marshal your evidence; you set forth testimony, experiences, and any documents you have. If the question is the ownership of property, you bring in the title deed. If it's the question of an accident, you bring in the testimony of doctors and eyewitnesses. These witnesses testify as to the nature of the accident—who caused it, how it occurred, the weather conditions, the road conditions.

Faith is the summation of all the evidence that would establish your case. It is the evidence, the proving, the conviction of things that are not seen.

You can't see some things, because faith reaches into an invisible world, but I assure you that underlying the reality of the pragmatic, visible world, there *is* an invisible world. Norman P. Grubb wrote a book titled *Touching the Invisible,* which was of great benefit to many Christians. With faith, we touch the invisible world, because Spirit underlies all the world that we live in.

Energy, Dr. Einstein and his colleagues have shown us, is the true reality. Taking the matter we can see and converting it back into energy releases fabulous force. The force behind the matter is a vastly superior power to the matter itself. Locked into the visible is an invisible reality, both in the scientific and spiritual realms.

Jesus Christ saw this invisible realm. He was aware of it, acquainted with it, and walked in it. The apostle Paul prayed that the eyes of our understanding might be enlightened; that we might know the hope of our calling and the exceeding riches of the Father; that we might understand the greatness of His power toward those of us who believe (*see* Ephesians 1:18).

These men had seen the invisible world. The apostle Paul was taken up into the third heaven. He heard sounds; he saw sights which were not lawful for men to talk about (*see* 2 Corinthians 12:2–4). There have been other people who have gone over the line— some in visions, some in trances, some even in physical death—and they've come back to tell us of this invisible world.

The whole premise of Christianity is that the Spirit world is enduring; the material, physical world is temporary. We live this life of seventy, eighty, ninety, or maybe one hundred years, but we look forward to eternal life, which will go on forever. Flesh and blood, which is subject to death, does not inherit this supernatural world of the Spirit. We realize that Spirit is eternal and powerful, while material, fleshy things are of lesser value.

I'm not saying that matter is evil, or our bodies are evil, *per se*. I am saying that they are weak and power-

less in comparison to the vast resources of the world of
the Spirit.

Faith penetrates into this invisible world and becomes our title deed to a claim on the Spirit world.
Faith is so powerful that if we make a proper claim
and marshal the proper evidence, we can bring forth
from the Spirit world enough power to move mountains. The Spirit of God and the Spirit of Jesus is the
source of power.

What do we do? Do we try to control God's power?
Of course not. Do we involve ourselves in some sort of
excursion into the "spirit world" of the occult? No, we
don't. This is forbidden by God's Word. This will lead
to evil, destruction, and confusion.

Instead, we submit ourselves to Jesus Christ, and
we submit ourselves to the perfect will of God. As we
flow in submission to the power of God, we begin to
find that His power is working for us, because we are
in tune with His power.

As an illustration: If you take a boat and put it into a
large river and begin to row upstream, you will find
yourself fighting constantly. You will be working
against the current. The current will do nothing for
you, but will be your enemy.

But if your journey coincides with the flow of the
river, then you find that you are being carried along by
a force which you cannot fully see, but which you
know is affecting your rate of progress.

This is what you and I must do in relation to God.

God, all-powerful, all-knowing, all-seeing, and all-loving, demands obedience. As we obey and submit ourselves to the course He has laid out for us, we will find miraculous things happening. His power is made available to us when we are going in the same direction He is. Our lives become part of His purpose.

So it isn't a question of saying to God, "I want something for me that is contrary to what You want." We say, "Father, I would like to see Your power demonstrated through me, in fulfillment of Your own wishes and desires." No one is going to find faith for anything that is contrary to the will of God.

As we pray "Increase our faith," or "Give us more faith," or "I pray for faith to believe in this," we must be submitted to the will of God. We must be in the will of God. We must understand the will of God.

I believe that the closing "Thy will be done" at the end of a prayer is nothing more or less than a faith killer. It is a way for you and me to justify our lack of faith.

I believe God wants us to know what His will is before we pray. He expects us to know—from His Word and His actions—what He likes and what He doesn't like, what He will do for us and what He will not do for us. When we understand, we have the warrant to go forth in faith and speak the word of faith, which brings about creative action.

When we go to the Word to find out where faith comes from, the apostle Paul tells us in Romans 10:17,

"So then faith cometh by hearing, and hearing by the word of God."

When we marshal our evidence, when we make our case for our own minds and spirits to enter into the world of God's power and resources—that invisible world of which I've been speaking—we must do so on the authority of the Word of God. What God has said in His Word is forever settled in heaven. If we know the Bible, if we know what the promises of God are, then we have faith.

Whenever faith comes, it must come through something that is tangible. The tangible reality of the promises of God are the foundation stone of faith. Faith, in turn, is the foundation of bringing about what we are hoping for from the invisible, the Word of God.

What type of things would Jesus Christ expect us, as His disciples, to see by faith? Jesus said one type of conduct was representative of great faith, and another was representative of little faith. Do you know what the Bible says is small faith; what caused Jesus to actually rebuke people?

Failure to walk on the water was a result of having little faith. Jesus Christ addressed Peter, who began to sink into the water as "O ye of little faith" (*see* Matthew 14:31). Failure to still a raging storm by the word of faith was worthy of a rebuke from Jesus Christ (*see* Mark 4:40; Luke 8:25). Failure to chase out a devil by the power of God brought not only a rebuke from Jesus, but a cry of dismay, ". . . O faithless and perverse generation . . . how long shall I suffer you? . . ." (Matthew 17:17).

On the other hand, there were at least two instances when Jesus commended people for having great faith. In one case, a Roman centurion, whose servant was sick, came to Jesus. The centurion said that he believed Jesus had the power to speak a word and heal the servant at a long distance. Jesus said, ". . . I have not found so great faith, no, not in Israel" (Luke 7:9).

The second instance dealt with a Syrophoenician woman whose daughter was demon-possessed. This woman was rebuked by Jesus, who told her that His mission was to the people of Israel, not to the Gentiles. She persisted, time and time again, despite discouragement and rebuke. She laid hold of the promise of God, and insisted that Jesus had the authority to do what she asked, and that if she persisted enough, she would have the reward.

Jesus gave her one of the supreme compliments: ". . . O woman, great is thy faith . . ." (Matthew 15:28). Needless to say, she received what she requested.

You and I stand before a God of the impossible. Faith begins with God, and Jesus Christ is the Author of our faith. He is the One who said, ". . . with God all things are possible" (Matthew 19:26). There is nothing that God cannot do. That which is thought impossible for man is possible for God.

God says if we want to enjoy an abundant life as

Christians, we are to come boldly to the throne of
grace to understand what His Word says, to abide in
Him, and to let His Word abide in us. If we do, we can
ask what we will, and it will be done for us. The nature of God and the power of His Word, living in us,
complement each other. One empowers the other,
bringing great faith, great victory, great miracles.

I want to pray that you might learn how to enjoy
faith as part of the abundant life.

Our heavenly Father, we pray that faith may descend as a
mantle from heaven upon each one of us. May the power of
the Holy Spirit touch our lives. Lord, increase all of our
faith, but let us learn to exercise the faith that You are giving us, that we might know Your Word and Your power.

Thank You, Father, as we appropriate the blessings of
Almighty God and reach out to enter into a fuller, more
abundant life in Jesus Christ.

This is my prayer for you.

6
Gift of God, Not of Works

No one can come before God on the final day and say, "I earned heaven. I earned a place in Your family. I earned a role as a child of God."

Have you ever had troubles? Have you wondered why your family wasn't behaving the way it should? Have you wished your relatives and in-laws were kinder to you? Have you had problems with your employer? Have you wondered why you were being persecuted? Have you wondered why there wasn't enough money to go around?

Every one of us, at one time or another, has encountered difficulties. Every one of us would like to know why there can't be more victory, why there can't be more help for those of us who are the children of the King of kings.

The reason we have not had the victory that God wants, and we have not lived in the abundance that He plans for us, is that we are ignorant of the truth of God's grace.

Let us then with confidence draw near to the throne of grace, that we may receive mercy and find grace to help in time of need.

Hebrews 4:16 RSV

You may say, "That's all very nice—grace. That's a theological term. Or is it what we say when we get ready to eat our supper? What's that got to do with my relationship to the boss?"

You haven't even begun to understand the meaning of grace! It is an amazing word. It's the word used to describe all of the gracious provision that God makes for His people.

In one instance it is unmerited favor. It is something that we did not earn, could not possibly buy, have no way of access to—except through the way God has provided. Yet over and over again, the Bible tells us that if we are children of God, we have access to grace.

"Let us then draw near with confidence to the throne of grace." The *throne* is God's very presence. God is spoken of in the Bible as sitting on a throne, a seat of power and influence.

The world has had its Alexanders, Napoleons, Caesars, Stalins, Hitlers, and Genghis Khans. But no throne of any authority, in any nation, can touch God's authority and power.

Jesus Christ said, ". . . All authority in heaven and on earth has been given to me. Go therefore . . ." (Matthew 28:18, 19 RSV). This means that there is no principality or ruler, however great or small, that is outside the scope of God's power. That's what God's throne means.

For those of us who are Christians, the throne of God is not a throne of terror. It is not a throne of judgment, or fear. It is a throne of grace, of unmerited favor. There, the Bible says, we may receive mercy and find grace to help in time of need.

Some may say, "But how does this figure in with what we say before dinner?" Frankly, what we say before dinner is a prayer, not grace. We have misused and misunderstood this term.

Grace implies the entire power of God Almighty, directed with loving concern toward His child or His church. Grace is what saves us, what keeps us, what protects us. Grace is what makes people like us, what gives us financial blessing, what heals us. Grace is what gives us the so-called charismatic gifts, the enablements for power.

Grace is what speaks to us when we move from place to place in service to the Lord. Grace is what goes before us and opens the door. Grace is what makes total strangers receptive to the Word of God. Grace is an attachment which God places upon His children to enable them to live a life of victory.

The apostle Paul told the Ephesians:

> For by grace are ye saved through faith; and that not of yourselves: it is the gift of God: Not of works, lest any man should boast.
>
> Ephesians 2:8, 9

Grace is unmerited, undeserved. There is no way a man can lay claim to it, other than by faith in Jesus Christ.

Each individual deserves help. Every individual has earned judgment. There is not one human being who is good—not one. Only God is good, and only His Son, Jesus Christ, lived a perfect life. Every other human being is guilty of sin.

Therefore, you and I have earned judgment, and you and I are incapable by ourselves of living a life which would warrant God's favor.

No one can come before God on the final day and say, "I earned heaven. I earned a place in Your family. I earned a role as a child of God."

This is why it is so ludicrous to hear people recite their good deeds as if they had a claim on heaven. All our so-called righteous deeds are as filthy rags in the sight of God.

Grace comes to us by faith. The fact that it comes by faith is in itself evidence of the grace of God. It flows from the throne of grace, the throne of love.

If indeed we can become reconciled with God by the death of His Son, how much more, now that we are part of His family, will He freely give us all things. This grace, for the Christian, is the access to a whole new realm of existence—one of victory, of abundant life, of blessing, and of miracles. None of these things is deserved.

It is a great mistake for our theologians and our preachers to exhort people to do good works so they can gain God's favor. God's favor flows from the

throne because of His nature, not because we can ever
earn it.

> Therefore being justified by faith, we have
> peace with God through our Lord Jesus Christ:
> By whom also we have access by faith into this
> grace wherein we stand, and rejoice in hope of
> the glory of God.
>
> Romans 5:1, 2

We have obtained our introduction into grace from
faith. By favor, God made grace available to us, and
He made faith available as a key to grace.

It is as if you are going along in the midst of a terrible hailstorm. Think of terrible, swirling, black
clouds, strong gusts of wind, hail pelting down, injur-
ing those who are in the midst of the storm.

Then suddenly, in the midst of all this darkness and
devastation, there is a spot of light. You run for the
light, and stand in it. In that light, there is no darkness,
no fear, no confusion. There is blessing, happiness,
and love. There is storm all around you, but you are
safe, standing in the light.

This is symbolic, in a limited sense, of the grace that
we stand in when we come to Jesus Christ and enter
into the family of God. As His children, it is not our
place to be in the maelstrom of the storm that swirls
around us. We do not have to be buffeted around by
all the torments that afflict the world.

I would be less than candid if I indicated that being a Christian frees us from difficulty. It does not necessarily take us away from all trouble, but even when trouble comes, the sunlight of God is shining, and there is peace upon us.

What are the benefits of grace? Eternal life is the greatest benefit. There is also the presence of Jesus Christ in our life. We walk with God and know Him. We understand His truth and His principles. He reveals His Word to us through the Holy Spirit, and gives us the gifts of the Holy Spirit.

The word for *grace* in the Bible is "charis." The word for *the gifts of the Spirit* is "charisma." *Charis* is grace. Special enablements of power are charisma, grace gifts. The ability to heal the sick is part of the charisma. Speaking through prophetic utterance is charisma. The power to work miracles is one more evidence of charisma.

Charis—grace. Charisma—an evidence of grace. The Greek word underlying the word *gifts* in the Bible is *grace*—the grace and favor of God. This is the grace we stand in when we come to Jesus Christ.

For that matter, all Christians should be charismatic. All Christians should stand in grace, and all should expect from God certain enablements of charisma that flow from the Holy Spirit of Almighty God.

In the Old Testament experience, we find the same thing, except there the word is *favor*. Grace and favor are the same thing. If the Ruler of all the world favors you, then He is giving you His power.

God favored a young man whose name was Joseph. Although at the age of sixteen he was sold into slavery by his jealous brothers, he still retained the favor of God. When he arrived on the slave block in Egypt, he was bought by a wealthy man named Potiphar.

Potiphar saw that the Lord was with Joseph, and that everything Joseph did prospered, so he made Joseph overseer over his house and all that he owned.

From the time he made Joseph overseer, the Lord blessed the Egyptian's house. This is an evidence of the material blessing that flows from God's favor.

No matter what happened to Joseph, he continued to walk with God in obedience to His Word. Even when he was thrown in jail on false charges, he prospered. The favor of God becomes the key to prosperity of every nature.

Our goal should be to win others to God, but the evidence that God is with us will come through the manifestation of His grace. It may be that God will hear and answer our prayers as evidence that He is with us.

In the case of Queen Esther, God gave her a special love for her husband. A favor that attached to Esther in turn projected itself into the heart of her husband. She was able to intercede for her entire nation, and to rescue them from a plot against them.

There is no way of knowing how this favor will

work, because there is no way of knowing the various ramifications that will occur. But the favor of the Lord will attach itself to everyone who loves God.

We should expect His favor. We should plead His favor. We should recognize His favor. We should stand in His favor.

Stephen was a witness for the Lord, and a witness for the Lord was often imprisoned, tortured, or killed. Stephen was willing to witness for Jesus Christ, even though it cost him his life.

We are told in the Book of Acts:

> And Stephen, full of faith and power, did great wonders and miracles among the people.
>
> Acts 6:8

The term *grace,* or *favor,* becomes almost synonymous with *power.* The favor of God produces power; it produces miracles; it produces wonders on behalf of the one with whom God is pleased.

God is pleased with His Son, Jesus Christ, and you and I are part of Him. We must realize that through the love of God, favor will come into our lives. It will be favor before the high and the mighty, favor with the lowly, with our wife or husband, with our children.

It will be the grace of God that brings about the blessing of God in the spiritual realm and in the material realm. We should stand in this favor and enjoy God's abundant life.

I would like to pray for every one of you, that you might know God's favor and know the throne of grace in your own life.

Father, we thank You for the grace of God in which we stand. We thank You for the throne of grace that we may approach to find grace in time of need. We thank You, Lord, that at Your throne, all things are possible, that at Your throne we only have *yea* and *amen*. We thank You that we have love, victory, joy, and peace in the Lord Jesus Christ.

Father, I pray for us all, that the favor of God may attach itself to us, that we might know Your grace. And I pray that we might come by faith to Jesus Christ, and having received Him as Saviour, might know the favor and blessing of Almighty God.

We thank You, Father, for this grace. We thank You for this favor. We thank You for the manifestations of Your Spirit.

Grant to Your people those enablements of power which will be pleasing in Thy sight, Father. In Jesus' name, *Amen.*

I am hoping and praying for you, that you might enjoy all aspects of God's abundant life.

Abba Eban, Israeli parliament member and former UN ambassador, is welcomed to CBN headquarters prior to a 700 Club interview. Eban, former Prime Minister Yitzhak Rabin, Shimon Peres, and other Israeli leaders have been Pat's guests as evidence of CBN's continuing interest in the prophetical events in Israel.

Laying the groundwork for a possible CBN broadcasting foothold to reach the Middle East, Pat met with Cypriot President Archbishop Makarios. The Reverend Chris Panos (left) and the Reverend Harald Bredesen accompanied Pat.

Bill Bright, president of the Campus Crusade for Christ International, and Pat talk about prayer as an essential force in their work.

Fulfilling Jesus' command to minister to those in prison, Pat pauses to pray for a prisoner during his visit to Florida State Prison. God's work in this prison and the impact of the visit by Pat and the 700 Club team was captured in the ninety-minute CBN television special "Maximum Security."

Demos Shakarian, Full Gospel Businessmen's Fellowship president, is no stranger to the 700 Club, being Pat's frequent guest.

Pat brings the message of the living Gospels to a record-breaking crowd at "Jesus '76" in Mercer, Pennsylvania.

Famed gospel singers, The Singing Rambos, discuss with
Pat the current music scene and the place of gospel music.
To the right of Pat are Dotty, Reba, and Buck Rambo. *Be-
low:* Joined in their lifework of evangelism, Pat meets with
Billy Graham at the National Religious Broadcasters Con-
vention in Washington, D.C.

Thousands of Americans were deeply moved by CBN's "It's Time to Pray, America" television special and pledged to pray during the forty days prior to the last presidential election. This special, the largest simultaneously released production from a Christian organization was available to 96 percent of the American people over 228 television stations, 300 radio stations, and Armed Forces Radio and Television Service.

Television as the tool of evangelism was the subject when Pat was visited by Rex Humbard, Christian broadcaster and pastor of "The Cathedral of Tomorrow." *Below:* This "Americas Now" telethon helped raise funds for CBN's first missionary radio station in Bogotá, Colombia.

In this picture taken several years ago, Pat and staff members Tom Wright and George Bunn operate controls at CBN studios in Portsmouth, Virginia.

7

Charter for Divine Guidance

Trust in the Lord with all thine heart; and lean not unto thine own understanding. In all thy ways acknowledge him, and he shall direct thy paths.

How many times have you wished that Jesus Christ could stand beside you and give you instruction concerning a decision you had to make? Wouldn't it be wonderful if this could happen?

If you are a Christian, it *should* happen. You should know what Jesus would say. You should have His guidance. You should know God's will.

I want to give you some principles concerning how you can enter into this aspect of the joy of His abundant life.

> Trust in the Lord with all thine heart; and lean not unto thine own understanding. In all thy ways acknowledge him, and he shall direct thy paths.
>
> Proverbs 3:5, 6

This is certainly a charter for divine guidance. This Scripture is His promise to us. However, this promise is conditioned on certain things, and I think you need to understand the conditions.

105

Trust in the Lord with all your heart. Your heart is the innermost part of you, the citadel of your personality, the core and motivation of your being. It is the deepest part of your spiritual life, the part that makes everything else tick—and that part of you must be centered totally on God.

David put it another way when he said, "My heart is fixed, O God . . ." (Psalms 57:7). If a ship is being guided by a directional instrument, that instrument must be fixed on a course, or the ship will be plowing through the sea in an aimless fashion. The guidance system of that ship must be fixed.

It will do you no good to have your heart fixed on personal wealth or other selfish motives, while at the same time you claim to have fixed it on God. Your heart must be zeroed in on one target—God Almighty—and the relationship must be one of absolute trust.

When I was in the U.S. Marine Corps, I was taught compass reading. It was a course that enabled me to lead a group of men from one point to another, in the dark, over unfamiliar terrain, merely by reference to a map and a compass.

My compass had to be fixed on magnetic north. I would have a map before me and would have to decide what variation from north would take me to my objective.

It was absolutely essential that I trusted my compass and map. I did not have the liberty to make variations in accordance with my personal preference.

I was told not to have the compass near any metallic object, which would pull the needle from true north. My compass needed to be free from any interference.

Just the same way, your heart must be fixed, and it must be in a relationship of trust with God. George Muller, the founder of several English orphanages, said, "When you see God's guidance, you must have no mind of your own in the matter."

That means you cannot be rooting for a particular outcome, hoping that God will say yes to something you want. You should be in a position of absolute dependence on Him, willing to go in trust wherever He says, because He is God Almighty.

The second rule of divine guidance is: *Do not lean on your own understanding.* If, while I was following a compass course, I began to follow a beautiful road that wandered off my course, I would miss my destination. The same would happen if I used my own intelligence to estimate the height of mountains or the difficulty of terrain. In a war situation, I could conceivably be killed, along with my men. I was not allowed to interject my own preferences, or try to second-guess the compass and map. My own knowledge was not adequate to meet the circumstances.

The same thing is true of divine guidance. You cannot lean on your own understanding. Neither you nor I has any knowledge of the future. We cannot, with any degree of certainty, say what will happen to us, to our surroundings, or to our world, one or twelve months hence. Only God Almighty knows what might happen.

That doesn't mean we forsake common sense or wisdom. It does mean we have to lean on God and then use the senses He has given us to aid us in moving from one place to another.

The third principle of divine guidance is: *In all your ways acknowledge Him.* What does that mean? It means you take into account the presence and authority of Almighty God in every aspect of your life. There is no way a person can dedicate one hour of faithful service to God a week, while he dedicates the remainder of the week to personal gain and pleasure. A man must take God Almighty into his business, into his home, and into his recreation.

In *all* your ways acknowledge Him. You cannot expect God to guide you in the issues that you regard as important, while at the same time you ignore Him in the little things. If you are not faithful in what is least, you will not be faithful in what is great. But if you are faithful in the little things in your life, then the Word of God says that you will be faithful in the great things.

Three necessary steps: Trust in the Lord with all your heart; do not lean on your own understanding; in all your ways acknowledge Him—and He shall direct your paths. He shall give you direction.

How will He guide you? Being sovereign, God can guide His children any way that He sees fit. From the overall understanding that we have of the Bible, of history, and of human experience, we can point out certain ways in which God may most likely express Himself.

Both the Old and New Testaments record supernatural visitations of God. The apostle Paul saw a vision of a man from Macedonia, saying, "Come over and help us." The apostle Peter had a vision and heard a voice saying to him, "What God hath cleansed, that call not thou common" (Acts 10:15). This led him to go with a Gentile sent from God. The other side of that story deals with Cornelius, the Gentile who went for Peter on instructions from God's angel.

Other instances have been viewed by people in the Bible as being of God. Someone would meet a particular person, who would say something or evidence knowledge that would seem to be God Almighty speaking. They would be sure that God had ordered the circumstance as a means of directing them.

One of the most extreme cases of God's guidance came about when a false prophet named Balaam was going against God's will, and his little donkey spoke to him (see Numbers 22:28–30).

An example of false guidance is the case of Jonah, who had been given specific instructions by God. Jonah found a ship bound in another direction, and

concluded that the ship was a providential circumstance enabling him to get out of an unpleasant
assignment.

We all know this was false guidance, and God
promptly brought Jonah back to his original assignment (*see* Jonah 1:1–17).

These are unusual events. I believe in visions,
dreams, and angels, but I do not believe that this is the
way God normally leads His children today.

How does He do it? He leads us through the Bible.

Thy word is a lamp unto my feet, and a light
unto my path.
                            Psalms 119:105

Wherewithal shall a young man cleanse his
way? by taking heed thereto according to thy
word.
                            Psalms 119:9

I frankly believe that about 98 percent of all the
guidance that you and I need is contained in the Bible. I believe that if we understand the Bible, we will
see Jesus. I believe that if we understand the Bible,
we will see the way of God. Almost every decision
that comes to us will be guided by Scripture, if we
have Scripture hidden in our hearts.

Thy word have I hid in mine heart, that I might
not sin against thee.
                            Psalms 119:11

If we have stored the Bible in our hearts, the Bible itself will guide us in almost every decision we have to make. This was the case with Timothy, a young man who met the apostle Paul, gave his heart to Jesus, and went into the ministry. Paul wrote to him:

> But continue thou in the things which thou hast learned and hast been assured of, knowing of whom thou hast learned them; And that from a child thou hast known the holy scriptures, which are able to make thee wise unto salvation through faith which is in Christ Jesus.
>
> 2 Timothy 3:14, 15

All Scripture is inspired by God and is profitable for teaching, for reproof, for correction, for training in righteousness. When you get right down to it, this takes in most types of guidance, doesn't it? If a person follows the law of God, the Word of God, he will have wisdom and knowledge of the ways of God. He'll order his affairs correctly.

A second major way God leads His people today is through the indwelling Holy Spirit. The prophet Isaiah wrote:

> And thine ears shall hear a word behind thee, saying, This is the way, walk ye in it . . . .
>
> Isaiah 30:21

The apostle Paul put it a little differently when he said, "And let the peace of God rule in your hearts . . ." (Colossians 3:15). Let the peace of God be a gyroscope in your life.

When you go to the left or right from the way that God has ordained for you, you will begin to sense disquiet. You will sense trouble, and you will know you are wrong. As long as the peace is there, you can go forth, confidently assured that your heart is fixed on the course that God has set for you. When the peace lifts, it is the Holy Spirit telling you, you are going in the wrong direction.

Greater guidance yet is the knowledge of God Himself.

The fear of the Lord is the beginning of wisdom: and the knowledge of the holy is understanding.

                                          Proverbs 9:10

I believe that if we know Jesus Christ—if we know Him as a person—we will begin to interact with Him. If we know God Almighty—if we in truth fear Him, and have knowledge of Him and His ways—we begin to interact with Him.

As we know Him, we will also know what He wants for us. We will know about the future. We will know how to make decisions today which will put us in a correct position for tomorrow. After all, what is wisdom? Wisdom is acting today as if you knew all about tomorrow. If we order our affairs according to the Word and knowledge of God, then we will indeed evidence wisdom.

This wisdom needs to be nurtured in a close relationship. We need to walk with God, to listen to God, to pray to God, to commune with Him, and to understand what He wants. We need Him, not just to go to in a crisis, crying, "God, give me guidance today," but all of the time.

The apostle Paul said: "Christ Jesus . . . is made unto us wisdom . . ." (1 Corinthians 1:30). He also said: ". . . we have the mind of Christ" (1 Corinthians 2:16). If a person has given his heart to Jesus, he has Jesus within him.

Jesus is the Author of all wisdom. He is the Guide. It isn't so much that we say, "God, give us guidance," but "God, I have *with me* the Guide." You don't need specific direction if your hand is placed in the hand of the One who can see everything.

Before long, as we grow in the life that God wants for us, our mind takes on more of the characteristics of His mind. That is what He meant when He said:

> . . . If ye abide in me, and my words abide in you, ye shall ask what ye will, and it shall be done unto you.
>
> John 15:7

If you want wisdom, God will give you wisdom. He will lead you in the way that you need to go, which is wisdom, because you are part of Him. You think like Him, and you react like Him. Because of this, His Spirit is upon you, and He is leading you.

This is part of our heritage in Christ, that we be led continuously. Indeed, even without our knowing it, His hand leads us, because we are part of His family.

I want to pray that you might enter into His wisdom and into His guidance. I want to pray that you might know personally the Guide who is the King of kings and Lord of lords.

Heavenly Father, at this moment we pray that our hearts might trust in You, that we might acknowledge You with all of our being. We pray that we might not lean on our own understanding, but that we lean and rest on Your Word. We pray that we might listen to the voice of Your Spirit, that we in truth be so surrendered to You that we have the mind of Christ. And we pray that the wisdom that comes from knowing You might operate in us.

Father, for every one of us, I pray for the power of God to come guide us, direct us, and bless us.

Thank You, Father, for this evidence of Your love. Thank You for the privileges we have. Thank You for the enjoyment of the abundant life in Jesus Christ. In His name, *Amen*.

This is my prayer for you.

8

Faith, Hope, and Love
Will Endure

"But when that which is perfect is come, then that which is in part shall be done away."

We live in a society of change. The manufacturers of this world have built everything to become obsolete. The cars that we drive, which seem so shiny and new today, are the stuff of tomorrow's junkyards. The fashions that we seek so eagerly are soon the dowdy numbers of yesterday.

Have you ever thumbed through the magazines of the 1930s? Have you looked at pictures of Victorian-age fashions? Have you gone to some of the inner cities and seen buildings which must have been magnificent in their day, but which are broken down and decaying?

If we are to possess things that are of significance, we must seek what is permanent. The Bible tells us that the fashion of this world is going to pass away, and whatever man thinks of as good is one day going to come to nothing. Even the showy evidences of God's power are going to terminate.

Only three attributes that God gives to us will survive:

118

So faith, hope, love abide, these three; but the greatest of these is love.

1 Corinthians 13:13 RSV

God says that if there are tongues, they will cease; if there is knowledge, it will be done away; if there are gifts or manifestations of prophecy, they will be done away. But, He says, love is never going to fail (*see* 1 Corinthians 13:8).

Faith, hope, and love have no end, because they partake of the nature of God Himself. They are characteristics of God, and therefore characteristics of the people who will be in heaven.

There are things here on earth that will never move into heaven. None of the churches we build will go to heaven. None of our schools and universities, none of the businesses at which we labor so hard, will be in heaven. It will be impossible to transmit bank accounts to heaven. Certainly our wardrobes, our automobiles, our vacation spots, and the other appurtenances of physical life cannot bridge the gap.

A good side of this is that some of our bad qualities won't go over, either. It will be impossible to carry along physical lust, because in heaven there will be no more physical bodies.

The failings of our mortal bodies will not go with us, nor can we carry along our strengths. The gifted athlete will have no superiority in heaven, and the cripple in the wheelchair will enter completely whole

into heaven. Many of the things that seem so important to us on earth will vanish in a moment.

If this is the case, a wise man would spend his time
and effort cultivating and acquiring those things
which endure. Even the marvelous manifestations of
God's grace, the charisma or charismatic manifestations, will be eliminated in heaven.

Why is this? It won't be necessary to speak in
tongues, because everybody will understand the
tongues of men and of angels. It will be unnecessary
to have prophetic messages, because everyone will
have a clear, open vision of Almighty God. We will
receive directly from Him all of the information we
need concerning the present and the future.

As for the word of wisdom or the word of knowledge, they will no longer be necessary, because we
will fully possess the mind of God. We will know Him
as He knows us. We will be like Him, for we will see
Him as He is. So that which is now seen through a
glass darkly will not be of any significance to us.

That doesn't mean these things aren't of great value
now—they are. We need these things to function in a
hostile environment, where we must demonstrate that
the God we serve is indeed the God of the supernatural, the God of eternity, and the Ruler of all men.
He visits His people with supernatural enablements,
which permit them to do the job He has assigned
them. Yet He says these tools will not be necessary in
heaven.

It is as if you were building a building. While it is under construction, you might need hoists, wheelbarrows, scaffolding, and various tools. Once the building is complete, these tools become superfluous. When the building is built, we take these tools away. They are surplus, no longer needed.

This is what the Bible tells us:

But when that which is perfect is come, then that which is in part shall be done away.

1 Corinthians 13:10

The perfect is Jesus Christ. When Jesus comes back, the building will be finished. The church, His Body, will be clothed in righteousness.

Therefore, the tools of building will not be needed any longer. Instead, the new graces, which will fill the temple, will endure and carry on.

Those three are faith, hope, and love. They will abide. They will continue on into heaven. The greatest of the three is love.

Several years ago, I decided that I wanted the greatest of God's gifts, so I set myself to pray for love. I said to God, "Lord, give me love. I must have love, for You are love."

God replied, "I am giving you hope."

I didn't want hope—I wanted love! So I complained, "God, I don't want hope. I want love."

God, in His gentle, gracious way, began to teach me His Word and to show me that the only way for me to have love was first to have hope. The only way that I could have hope was to have trials.

I didn't want trials. I didn't want trouble. I wanted love! Love is fun. Love is good.

But God said, "No, that's not the way you get love. Love must come through trials."

If we are going to have the things that endure, if we are to experience the abundance of life in this world and the next, we must realize that a gracious God, in order to perfect us, must from time to time place us in difficult circumstances to perfect those attributes which will endure in heaven.

In the Book of Romans, the apostle Paul speaks of these things:

> Therefore being justified by faith, we have peace with God through our Lord Jesus Christ: By whom also we have access by faith into this grace wherein we stand, and rejoice in hope of the glory of God. And not only so, but we glory in tribulations also: knowing that tribulation worketh patience; and patience, experience; and experience, hope: And hope maketh not ashamed; because the love of God is shed abroad in our hearts by the Holy Ghost which is given unto us.
>
> Romans 5:1–5

We glory (rejoice) in tribulation. Tribulation isn't pleasant. It means people say unkind things about us. It means we may not have all the money we need. It may mean that we have physical suffering.

It may mean that we're put, as I was, in a difficult place. I was not seeing the fulfillment of my desires. I was crowded into one of the most wretched slums in America.

Tribulation—it comes in all sizes and all packages. It isn't as bad as it sounds, for tribulation brings patience.

The Greek word for *patience* in this particular instance is "hupŏmŏnē." It means, "to get under a burden and hold up under it." Another translation for it is "perseverance."

You can see somebody holding a burden in an uncomfortable situation, and he is groaning under it. The Christian doesn't quit. He doesn't run away. He doesn't curse God. He doesn't complain and question God's goodness. He learns perseverance.

But what does this do? Perseverance brings about experience—proven character. The Bible says it is good to bear the yoke in your youth (*see* Lamentations 3:27). Many young men have assumed responsibilities and carried them without complaining, without being dishonest, and without cheating. As they carried the load, they developed character. They can be relied upon.

The Bible says that to put faith in somebody who will not bear the load is like having a leg out of joint (*see* Proverbs 25:19). Try to rest on that leg, and it will cause you to fall and stumble. You need people who are tried and tested, and God lets tribulation happen to us to perfect our character. There is no other way to do it, or He would use it.

When character develops, the person begins to realize that he didn't break under the load. In my brief sojourn in Bedford-Stuyvesant, New York, I found that I didn't contract an awful disease, go hungry, or become a victim of crime. I did very nicely.

It certainly was not a paradise, but as I lived there, I realized that God was there with me. I began to develop hope in God, because I saw that He was faithful. I began to know His peace and to hope in Him.

Before long, He took me out of there and gave me something else. Then he moved me again, into something better. So it went, in progressive steps. He put me in a difficult situation and then lifted me into a better one.

Each time, I would find that I had more hope in God and in His goodness. I could say, "I trust God. I know, beyond a shadow of a doubt, that God is faithful. I trust Him, because I have seen His hand at work over and over again."

This is the kind of experience that brings about

character—the character of somebody who is steady, who knows that he knows.

If everything in your life is easy, there is no way that you will learn how God can provide for you. Whatever your security blanket is, how will you know whether or not God is faithful when the security blanket is removed?

There is only one way to know, and that is to be with God without the security, in a difficult situation, with hope. When hope rises in your life, you do not have to try to grab something for yourself. If you live in a house, and you feel that is the only house you will ever have, you fight to keep that house. But if God has taken you into ten houses, and never failed you in any of them, then you know He can provide an eleventh.

If someone comes along and needs a house, you wouldn't be terribly disturbed to give him yours, knowing that God has a better one somewhere else for you.

This is the fabric of love, because love is concern for other people. Love is a willingness to give of yourself, of your possessions, of your time, without saying, "If I don't get it for me, I won't have any."

This doesn't come about overnight. It is a process that God starts in us when we find the Lord Jesus as our Saviour, and He brings out of us when we go to be with Him in glory. This is part of life, because God is building something permanent in us. He is polishing and perfecting us to make us like Jesus.

We can't ever say we "have it made," because we are not made. We are always in a state of change, and God is always making us more and more like Jesus. There are times when He must put us in the fire to purify us and cause us to have more hope, so we might have more love.

I found this to be true in Korea. First I served in a replacement-training command in Japan. Then I served at division headquarters rear echelon in Korea. Then I was with the forward command post, right next to the battlefield.

A most interesting thing took place during this experience. The farther away we were from the battle line, the more selfish the men and officers became. The closer they came to the ultimate reality of the bullet that might send them into eternity, the more generous, compassionate, and concerned for each other they became.

God recognizes this, and He perfects it in us. He says that these enduring things are fruits of the Holy Spirit. They are not something we think of ourselves, for it is impossible for us to take on the attributes of God on our own.

They are called fruits, but fruit is something that develops over a period of time.

> But the fruit of the Spirit is love, joy, peace, patience, kindness, goodness, faithfulness, gentleness, self-control . . . .
>
> Galatians 5:22, 23 RSV

If we analyze these nine fruits of the Holy Spirit, we would find faith, hope, and love central in them. These are the attributes of Jesus Christ, and Jesus lives forever. They are the fruits of the indwelling Christ. He perfects Himself in us.

The gifts of the Holy Spirit are the life of Jesus Christ in ministry for power. When the ministry is over, we need His life—love, joy, peace, patience, kindness, goodness, faithfulness, gentleness, self-control. Against such things, there is no law.

I desire that every one of you should have the life of Jesus Christ within you. The apostle Paul wrote: "My little children, of whom I travail in birth again until Christ be formed in you" (Galatians 4:19). If we are going to know the joy of the abundant life in Christ, we must open ourselves to the working of God. He starts with faith. The trying of that faith leads to hope. Hope makes us not ashamed, because through hope in God, the love of God is spread abroad in our hearts by the Holy Spirit, who is given unto us.

Our heavenly Father, at this moment we pray for every one of us, that we might know faith, hope, and love, for we know they will endure beyond the grave into eternity.

Lord, we want that which is greatest of all. Give us love, Father, for Thee. Give us love for one another.

Whatever is necessary to perfect that love within us, do it, Father. May Your Holy Spirit work that thing which is pleasing in Your sight, that Jesus Christ might be formed within us and glorified within His church. We ask these things in His name. *Amen.*

This is my prayer for you. God bless you.